FRESH COURAGE TAKE

FRESH COURAGE TAKE

Duncan B Heriot

THE SAINT ANDREW PRESS
EDINBURGH

© Duncan B Heriot

First published in 1968 by
THE DRUMMOND TRUST
Republished in 1984, 1990 by
THE SAINT ANDREW PRESS
121 George Street
Edinburgh EH2 4YN

ISBN 0 7152 0575 7

*Publisher's Note: Biblical quotations which appear in
italics are taken from the King James (or Authorized) Version.*

*The Publisher acknowledges financial assistance from
The Drummond Trust
towards the publication of this volume.*

This book has been set in 11/12 pt Palatino.
Cover design by Mark Blackadder.
Printed and Bound in Great Britain by
Athenaeum Press Ltd., Newcastle upon Tyne.

FOREWORD
(*to the original edition*)

The generous reception of *The Hospital Bedside Book* has led to a request for a companion volume that would further aim at bringing comfort and help to human hearts.

All of us at times have had occasion to visit friends who are lying sick at home or in hospital. Usually we take to them gifts of flowers or 'sweets' as tangible tokens of our affection. But flowers fade and 'sweets' are consumed. Many have found that invalids value the gift of *The Hospital Bedside Book*, for, unlike the temporal gifts that vanish, the words of uplift therein are based on the eternal verities.

The Poetry, Readings and Prayers in *The Hospital Bedside Book* were chosen with the particular aim of helping those who were sick in mind or body. In this volume the scope has been widened to include other occasions when the human heart cries out for help.

May I suggest that the best way to use this book is to read a section slowly and thoughtfully, memorise a sentence or two, then lie back and meditate on them. If the book is thus used, the reader will find that in a remarkably short space of time, he (or she) has stored his mind with many helpful thoughts and provided himself with an inner strength of spirit.

D B Heriot

AUTHOR'S NOTE
(from *The Hospital Bedside Book*)

The prayers (herein) have been chosen from those composed by 'Saints of God' down the centuries. To avoid infringing copyright none has been taken from the many inspiring 'Books of Prayers' by modern writers, but if anywhere in the book I have so infringed, I would crave forgiveness in view of the purpose for which it has been compiled.

D B Heriot

Fresh Courage Take was in the Publisher's hands when my brother died on the 29th April 1967. I wish here to acknowledge my great indebtedness to the late Revd Andrew McCosh, MA , STM, of the Stirling Tract Enterprise, for his wise counsel and guidance in helping me with the original publishing of my brother's book.

Miss B Heriot

FRESH COURAGE TAKE

Ye fearful saints, fresh courage take;
The clouds ye so much dread
Are big with mercy, and shall break
In blessings on your head.

William Cowper, 1731-1800

'Lord, teach us to pray.'

The Lord's Prayer

Our Father, which art in Heaven,
Hallowed be thy Name.
Thy Kingdom come.
Thy will be done
In Earth, as it is in Heaven.
Give us this day our daily bread.
And forgive us our trespasses,
As we forgive them that trespass against us,
And lead us not into temptation;
But deliver us from evil;
For thine is the Kingdom,
The Power and the Glory,
For ever and ever. Amen.

FIRST DAY

Thy word have I hid in mine heart. (Psalm 119:11)
Thy word is a lamp at my feet, and a light unto my
path. (Psalm 119:105)
Let the word of Christ dwell in you richly in all wisdom.
(Colossians 3:16)

> Thy Word is like a garden, Lord,
>   With flowers bright and fair;
> And everyone who seeks may pluck
>   A lovely garland there.
> Thy Word is like a deep deep mine;
>   And jewels rich and rare
> Are hidden in its mighty depths,
>   For every searcher there.
> Thy Word is like a starry host;
>   A thousand rays of light
> Are seen to guide the traveller
>   And make his pathway bright.

Edwin Hodder, 1837-1904

Daily Reading
(selected verses from the Scriptures)

Open thou mine eyes, that I may behold wondrous things out of thy law.

The entrance of thy words giveth light; it
giveth understanding to the simple.

For whatsoever things were written afore-

1

time were written for our learning, that we through patience and comfort of the Scriptures might have hope.

For the gospel came not unto you in word only. The Word was made flesh and dwelt among us, and we beheld his glory, the glory as of the only begotten of the Father, full of grace and truth.

Prayers
In the morning
O God, who hast folded back the mantle of the night to clothe us in golden glory of the day, chase from our hearts all gloomy thoughts, and make us glad with the brightness of hope, that we may effectively aspire to unwon virtues; through Jesus Christ our Lord. Amen.

Ancient Collect, 590

In the evening
O gracious God and most merciful Father, who hast given us the rich and precious jewel of thy Holy Word: assist us with thy Spirit, that it may be written in our hearts to our everlasting comfort, to re-form us according to thine own image and increase in us all heavenly virtues; for Jesus Christ's sake. Amen.

Edward VI, 1537-1553

Blessed Lord, who hast caused all Holy Scriptures to be written for our learning: grant that we may in such wise hear them, read, mark, learn, and inwardly digest them, that by patience, and comfort of thy Holy Word, we may embrace and ever hold fast the blessed hope of everlasting life, which thou hast given us in our Saviour Jesus Christ. Amen.

The First Prayer Book of Edward VI, 1549

Lord, open thou our eyes, that we may behold wondrous things out of thy law.

Psalm 119:18

SECOND DAY

This is the day which the Lord hath made; we will rejoice and be glad in it. (Psalm 118:24)

Rejoice! the Lord is King;
    Your Lord and King adore;
Mortals, give thanks and sing,
    And triumph evermore:
Lift up your heart, lift up your voice:
Rejoice! again I say, rejoice.

Charles Wesley, 1707-1788

Daily Reading
Psalm 100 (Scottish metrical version)

All people that on earth do dwell,
    Sing to the Lord with *cheerful* voice;
Him serve with *mirth*, his praise forth tell;
    Come ye before him and *rejoice*.

The Lord, ye know, is God indeed:
    Without our aid he did us make;
We are his flock, he doth us feed;
    And for his sheep, he doth us take.

O enter then his gates with praise,
    Approach with joy his courts unto;
Praise, laud, and bless his name always,
    For it is seemly so to do.

For why, the Lord our God is good;
    His mercy is for ever sure;
His truth at all times firmly stood,
    And shall from age to age endure.

William Kethe, c. 1550-1600

Prayers
In the morning

Grant us, O Lord, to pass this day away in gladness and peace, without stumbling and without stain; that reaching the eventide victorious over all temptation, we may praise thee, the eternal God, who dost govern all things world without end. Amen.

Mozarabic Liturgy, c. 600

O God, as the day returns and brings us the pretty round of irritating duties, help us perform them with laughter and kind faces; let cheerfulness abound with industry. Give us to go blithely on our business all this day, bring us to our resting beds weary and content and undishonoured, and grant us in the end the gift of sleep. We ask this in the name of Jesus Christ our Lord. Amen.

R L Stevenson, 1850-1894

In the evening
Lord, as we look back at what we have said and done this day, grant that we may be able to take pleasure therein. May it all be fit for thine eye to see. Give us enthusiasm to do our daily tasks, patience in performing, and cheerfulness in doing them. Where we are called to do work that seems to us monotonous and dreary, may we think of it as thy task, and make what is unlovely beautiful through loving service, so that at the close of day we may lie down content, at peace with ourselves, at peace with others and at peace with thee; for thy name's sake. Amen.

George Dawson, 1821-1876 (adapted)

THIRD DAY

The eternal God is thy refuge and underneath are the everlasting arms. (Deuteronomy 33:27)

Other refuge have I none;
Hangs my helpless soul on thee;
Leave, ah! leave me not alone,
Still support and comfort me:
All my trust on thee is stayed;

All my help from thee I bring;
Cover my defenceless head
With the shadow of thy wing.

Charles Wesley, 1707-1788

Daily Reading
Psalm 46 (selected)

God is our refuge and strength, a very present help in trouble.

Therefore we will not fear, though the earth be removed, and though the mountains be carried into the midst of the sea;

Though the waters thereof roar and be troubled, though the mountains shake with the swelling thereof.

The Lord of hosts is with us; the God of Jacob is our refuge.

Come, behold the works of the Lord. He maketh wars to cease to the end of the earth; he breaketh the bow, and cutteth the spear in sunder; he burneth the chariot in the fire.

Be still and know that I am God: I will be exalted among the heathen, I will be exalted in the earth.

The Lord of hosts is with us; the God of Jacob is our refuge.

Prayers
In the morning

Almighty God, Lord of the storm and of the calm, the vexed sea and the quiet haven, of day and night, of life and of death; grant unto us so to have our hearts stayed upon thy faithfulness, thine unchangingness and love, that whosoever betide us, however black the cloud or dark the night, with quiet faith trusting in thee, we may abide all storms and troubles of this mortal life, beseeching thee that they may turn to our soul's good. We ask for thy mercy's sake, shown in Jesus Christ our Lord. Amen.

George Dawson, 1821-1876

In the evening

O thou who knowest our hearts, and who seest our temptations and struggles, have pity upon us, and deliver us from sins which make war upon our souls. Thou art all-powerful, and we are weak and erring. Our trust is in thee, O God. Deliver us from the bondage of evil, and grant that we may be thy devoted servants, serving thee in the freedom of holy love, for Christ's sake. Amen.

Eugene Bersier, 1831-1889

Grant unto us, we beseech thee, O Almighty God, that we, who seek the shelter of thy protection, being defended from all evils, may serve thee in peace and quietness of spirit; through Jesus Christ our Lord. Amen.

Roman Breviary

FOURTH DAY

He is able to save them to the uttermost that come unto God by him. (Hebrews 7:25)

Jesus, thou joy of loving hearts,
Thou Fount of life, thou light of men;
From the best bliss that earth imparts,
We turn unfilled to thee again.

Thy truth unchanged hath ever stood;
Thou savest those that on thee call;
To them that seek thee thou art good,
To them that find thee, all in all!

Bernard of Clairvaux, twelfth century
(trans. Ray Palmer, 1808-1887)

Daily Reading
Luke 23 (selected)

And there were also two other malefactors, led with him to be put to death. And when they were come to the place, which is called Calvary, there they crucified him, and the malefactors, one on the right hand and the other on the left.

Then said Jesus, Father forgive them; for they know not what they do.

And one of the malefactors which were hanged railed on him, saying, If thou be the Christ, save thyself and us.

But the other answering rebuked him, saying, Dost not thou fear God, seeing thou art in the same condemnation? And we indeed justly; for we receive the due reward of our deeds; but this man hath done nothing amiss.

And he said unto Jesus, Lord remember me when thou comest into thy Kingdom.

And Jesus said unto him, Verily, I say unto thee, Today shalt thou be with me in paradise.

Prayers
In the morning

O Lord God, we wish that our lives had in them nothing unclean; nothing to make us ashamed. We know what is pure and good, yet there oftimes comes to us some grovelling after evil, some wandering after sin, some falling into temptation. Forgive us, our Father, wherein we have erred. Let our lives be all of a piece with our best desires. Give us that quiet indwelling trust in thee which colours all things and leads us in everything we think or do. We offer this prayer in Christ's name. Amen.

George Dawson, 1821-1876 (adapted)

In the evening

Almighty and merciful God, who knowest the thoughts of our hearts, we confess we have sinned against thee. Wash us, we beseech thee, from the stains of our past sins, and give us grace and power to put away all hurtfull things, so that, being delivered from the bondage of sin, we may bring forth worthy fruits of repentance.

O Eternal Light, shine into our hearts. O Eternal Goodness, deliver us from evil. O Eternal Power, be thou our support. Eternal Wisdom, scatter the darkness of our ignorance. Eternal Pity, have mercy upon us. Grant unto us, that with all our hearts and minds, and strength, we may evermore seek thy face; through Jesus Christ, our only Saviour and Redeemer. Amen.

Albinus Flaccus Alcuinus, 735-804,
Yorkshire priest and scholar; advisor to Charlemagne.

FIFTH DAY

The Lord is the strength of my life; of whom shall I be afraid? (Psalm 27:1)

God is my strong salvation.
    What foe have I to fear?
In darkness and temptation
    My light, my help is near.

Though hosts encamp around me,
    Firm to the fight I stand:
What terror can confound me,
    With God at my right hand?

James Montgomery, 1771-1854

Daily Reading
Psalm 91 (selected)

He that dwelleth in the secret place of the most High shall abide under the shadow of the Almighty.

I will say of the Lord, he is my refuge and my fortress: my God; in him I will trust.

Surely he shall deliver thee from the snare of the fowler, and from the noisome pestilence.

He shall cover thee with his feathers and under his wings shalt thou trust: his truth shall be thy shield and buckler.

Thou shalt not be afraid for the terror by night: nor for arrow that flieth by day; nor for the pestilence that walketh in darkness; nor for the destruction that wasteth at noon-day.

Because thou has made the Lord, even the most High, thy habitation; there shall no evil befall thee, neither shall any plague come nigh thy dwelling. For he shall give his angels charge over thee, to keep thee all in thy ways.

Prayers
In the morning

O Lord God, in whom we live and move and have our being, open our eyes that we may behold thy Fatherly presence ever about us. Teach us to be anxious for nothing, and when we have done what thou hast given us to do, help us, O God our Saviour, to leave the issue to thy wisdom, knowing that all things are possible to us through thy Son our Saviour, Jesus Christ. Amen.

R M Benson, 1825-1915

O God, the Father everlasting, who in thy wondrous grace, standest within the shadows, keeping watch over thine own; grant that in every peril and perplexity, in our groping and weariness, we may know the comfort of thy pervading Presence. When the day grows dark may we fear no evil because thy hand is upon us. Lead us onwards through the darkness into thy light, through the sorrows into the joy of the Lord, and through the Cross of Sacrifice into closer communion with thy Son, ever Jesus Christ our Lord. Amen.

Dr John Hunter, 1849-1917

Grant we beseech thee, Almighty God, that we in our tribulation may yet be of good cheer and because of thy loving-kindness find thee mighty to save from all dangers; through Jesus Christ. Amen.

Roman Breviary

SIXTH DAY

Be strong and of a good courage; be not afraid, neither be thou dismayed; for the Lord thy God is with thee whithersoever thou goest. (Joshua 1:9)

Courage brother ! do not stumble,
 Though thy path be dark as night;
There's a star to guide the humble:
 'Trust in God, and do the right'.

Though the road be rough and dreary,
　　And its end far out of sight;
Foot it bravely; strong or weary,
　　Trust in God, and do the right.

Norman Macleod, 1812-1872

Daily Reading
Ephesians 6 (selected)

Finally, my brethren, be strong in the Lord, and in the power of his might.

Put on the whole armour of God, that ye may be able to stand against the wiles of the devil. For we wrestle not against flesh and blood, but against principalities, against powers, against the rulers of the darkness of this world.

Wherefore take unto you the whole armour of God, that ye may be able to withstand in the evil day, and having done all, to stand. Above all, taking the shield of faith, wherewith ye shall be able to quench all the fiery darts of the wicked. And take the helmet of salvation, and the sword of the spirit, which is the Word of God.

Prayers
In the morning

O Almighty God, grant, we beseech thee, that we whose trust is under the shadow of thy wings, may, through the help of thy power, overcome difficulties, temptations and all evils that rise up against us this day; through Jesus Christ our Lord. Amen.

Roman Breviary

13

We confess unto thee, O God, how weak we are in ourselves, how powerless to do the work of life, how prone to selfishness and sin. We ask thee to grant us the strength of thy Spirit. Enable us to repress every selfish inclination, every wilful purpose, every unkind feeling, every deed of anger and impatience, and to cherish love, constant kindness, to think pure thoughts and to do generous and helpful deeds; for Christ's sake we ask it. Amen.

Thomas T Stone, 1801-1895

In the evening
Blessed Lord, who wast tempted in all things like as we are, have mercy upon our frailty. Out of weakness give us strength. Support us in time of temptation. Embolden us in times of danger. Help us to do thy work with good courage; and to continue thy faithful soldiers and servants unto our life's end; for thy name's sake. Amen.

Bishop Westcott, 1825-1901

SEVENTH DAY

When thou liest down, thou shalt not be afraid; yea, thou shalt lie down, and thy sleep shall be sweet. (Proverbs 3:24)

Sleep Sweet

Within this quiet room,
O Friend, whoe'er thou art,

And let no mournful yesterdays
Disturb thy peaceful heart;
Nor let tomorrow scare thy rest
With dreams of coming ill,
Thy Maker is thy changeless friend,
His love surrounds thee still.
Forget thyself and all thy woes,
Put out each feverish light;
The stars are watching overhead,
Sleep sweet, Goodnight, Goodnight.

Daily Reading
Psalms 4 and 42 (selected)

As the hart panteth after the water brooks, so panteth my soul after thee, O God. My soul thirsteth for God, for the living God.

Why art thou cast down, O my soul? And why art thou disquieted within me? Hope thou in God: for I shall yet praise him for the help of his countenance.

Lord, lift thou up the light of thy countenance upon me.

Thou hast put gladness in my heart.

I will both lay me down in peace and sleep: for thou, Lord, only makest me to dwell in safety.

Prayers
In the morning

Grant calmness and control of thoughts to those who are facing uncertainty and anxiety; let their hearts stand fast, believing in the Lord. Amen.

Russian Liturgy

O Lord, this is our desire—to walk along the path of life thou hast appointed us in steadfastness of faith; and because outward events have so much power to disturb our inward peace, do thou, Gracious Lord, calm and settle our souls. Let not the cares or duties of life press on us too heavily; but lighten our burdens, that we may follow thy way in quietness; through Jesus Christ our Lord. Amen.

Maria Hare, 1798-1870 (adapted)

In the evening

Now as the day draws to an ending, let thy peace descend upon us, and on our homes. Take from us all irksome and doleful thoughts; still every fear; that we may trustfully give ourselves into thy keeping, and say, 'I will lay me down and sleep; for thou, Lord, only makest me to dwell in safety'. Amen.

Dr James Ferguson

Almighty God, who seest that we have no power of ourselves to help ourselves; keep us both outwardly in our bodies, and inwardly in our souls; that we may be defended from all adversities which may happen to the body, and from all evil thoughts which may assault and hurt the soul; through Jesus Christ our Lord. Amen.

Gregorian Sacramentary, 590

EIGHTH DAY

Do not be anxious about tomorrow.
(Matthew 6:34, RSV)
God shall supply all your need. (Philippians 4:19)
In quietness and confidence shall be your strength.
(Isaiah 30:15)

For life and love, for rest and food,
　　For daily help and nightly care,
Sing to the Lord, for he is good,
　　And praise his name, for it is fair.

For strength to those who on him wait,
　　His truth to prove, his will to do,
Praise ye our God, for he is great;
　　Trust in his Name, for it is true.

J S B Monsell, 1811-1875

Daily Reading
(selected verses from the Psalms)

O God, be not far from me, for trouble is near.

The Lord is a refuge in time of trouble.

Cast thy burden upon the Lord, and he shall sustain thee.

What time I am afraid I will trust in thee.

In God have I put my trust: I will not be afraid.

Mine eyes are unto thee, O God, the Lord: in thee is my trust; leave not my soul destitute; for thou art my hope; O Lord God.

The Lord is my rock, and my fortress, and my deliverer; my God, my strength, in whom I will trust.

The Lord is a shield to all that trust in him.

He is their strength in time of trouble, none that trust in him shall be desolate.

Blessed is the man that maketh the Lord his trust.

Prayers
In the morning
Most merciful God, the Helper of all men, so strengthen us by thy power that our fears and our sorrows may be turned into joy; through Jesus Christ our Lord. Amen.

Sarum Breviary, 1085

O Lord, who in infinite wisdom and love orderest all things for thy children, in thy tender pity order everything this day for me. Thou, who madest me knowest my weakness. Lord, I know thou wilt lay no greater burden on me than thou canst help me to bear. Teach me to receive all things this day as from thee; grant me in all things to please thee; bring me through all things nearer unto thee; bring me day by day nearer to thyself. Amen.

E B Pusey, 1800-1882

In the evening
Grant unto us, Almighty God, the peace that passeth understanding; that we, amid the storms and troubles of this life, may rest in thee, knowing that all things are under thy care, governed by thy will, guarded by thy love; so that with a quiet heart we may be unafraid of

the storms of life, the cloud and the thick darkness; ever rejoicing to know that the darkness and the light are both alike to thee. Guide, guard and govern us even to the end, that none of us may fail to lay hold upon immortal life; through Jesus Christ our Lord. Amen.

George Dawson, 1821-1876

NINTH DAY

Render unto God the things which be God's.
(Luke 20:25)

Be thou my vision, O Lord of my heart,
Be all else but naught to me, save that thou art;
Be thou my best thought in the day and the night,
Both waking and sleeping, thy presence my light.

Be thou my wisdom, be thou my true word;
Be thou ever with me, and I with thee, Lord;
Be thou my great Father, and I thy true son;
Be thou in me dwelling, and I with thee one.

Be thou my breastplate, my sword for the fight;
Be thou my whole armour, be thou my true might;
Be thou my soul's shelter, be thou my strong tower,
O raise thou me heavenward, great power of my power.

Ancient Irish

Daily Reading
Romans 12 (selected)

I beseech you therefore, brethren, by the mercies of God, that ye present your bodies a living sacrifice, consecrated to God and worthy of his acceptance; this is the worship due from you as rational creatures.

Be kindly affectioned one to another with brotherly love; in honour preferring one another.

Not slothful in business; aglow with the Spirit; serving the Lord.

Rejoicing in hope; patient in affliction; persevering in prayer; providing generously for the needs of others; giving the stranger a loving welcome.

Prayers
In the morning

Let thy tender mercy, O Lord, enfold the sick and suffering. O God, who seest that our cheerfulness is the companion of our strength, but in time of weakness, quick to take wings and fly away; lay no more upon thy suffering children than they are able to bear, but temper every trial to the measure of their endurance. Let those who are afflicted know that in quietness and confidence is their strength. Give them a calm trust that thou doest all things well. In thy good time and way grant them to regain health and gladness, through the love and power of our Saviour Jesus Christ. Amen.

Roland Williams, 1818-1870

In the evening

O God our Father, before we go to rest we would commit ourselves to thy loving care, beseeching thee to forgive us for all our sins this day, and to keep alive thy grace in our hearts. Cleanse us from all sin, pride, harshness, and selfishness, and give us the spirit of meekness, humility, and love. O Lord our God, keep thyself ever present to us and perfect thy strength in our weakness. Take us and ours under thy blessed care this night and evermore; through Jesus Christ our Lord. Amen.

Thomas Arnold, 1795-1842 (adapted)

TENTH DAY

This man receiveth sinners. (Luke 15:2)

Come and rejoice with me!
I, once so sick at heart,
Have met with One who knows my case,
And knows the healing art

Come and rejoice with me!
For I was wearied sore,
And I have found a mighty arm
Which holds me evermore.

Come and rejoice with me!
For I have found a Friend
Who knows my hearts most secret depths
Yet loves me without end.

Elizabeth R Charles, 1828-1896

Daily Reading
Matthew 9:10-13 and Luke 15:7

And it came to pass, as Jesus sat at meat in the house, behold, many publicans and sinners came and sat down with him.

And when the Pharisees saw it, they said unto his disciples, Why does your master eat with publicans and sinners?

But when Jesus heard that, he said unto them, They that be whole need not a physician, but they that are sick. I am not come to call the righteous, but sinners to repentance.

I say unto you, that joy shall be in heaven over one sinner that repenteth, more than over ninety and nine just persons, which need no repentance.

Prayers
In the morning

Grant, we beseech thee, merciful Lord, to thy faithful people pardon and peace, that they may be cleansed from all their sins, and serve thee with a quiet mind; through Jesus Christ our Lord. Amen.

Gelasian Sacramentary, 494

Almighty God, unto whom all hearts are open, all desires known, and from whom no secrets are hid; cleanse the thoughts of our hearts by the inspiration of thy Holy Spirit, that we may perfectly love thee, and worthily magnify thy holy name; through Jesus Christ our Lord. Amen.

Gregorian Sacramentary, 590

In the evening
O God, our sins are many; strip us of them like a garment.

Sumerian poet, about 2000 BC, from a cuneiform inscription found at Akkad.

All that we ought to have thought and have not thought,
    All that we ought to have said and have not said,
    All that we ought to have done and have not done;
    All that we ought not to have thought and yet have thought,
    All that we ought not to have spoken and yet have spoken,
    All that we ought not to have done and yet have done,
    For thoughts, words and works, we repent O God, and ask for forgiveness.

The Zendavesta

ELEVENTH DAY

Thou, Lord, art good, and ready to forgive; and plenteous in mercy unto all them that call upon thee. (Psalm 86:5)

Hark the glad sound! the Saviour comes,
    The Saviour promised long;
Let every heart prepare a throne,
    And every voice a song.

23

He comes, the prisoner to release,
   In Satan's bondage held:
The gates of brass before him burst
   The iron fetters yield.

He comes, the broken heart to bind,
   The bleeding soul to cure,
And with treasures of his grace
   To enrich the humble poor.

Philip Doddridge, 1702-1751

Daily Reading
Psalm 32 (selected)

Blessed is he whose transgression is forgiven, whose sin is covered.

Blessed is the man unto whom the Lord imputeth not iniquity, and in whose spirit there is no guile.

I acknowledge my sin unto thee, and mine iniquity have I not hid. I said, I will confess my transgressions unto the Lord; and thou forgavest the iniquity of my sin.

Thou art my hiding place; thou shalt preserve me from trouble; thou shalt compass me about with songs of deliverance.

Prayers
In the morning

We beseech thee, that thou wilt forgive us our selfishness, and our pride, and our sordidness, and our abandonment of things spiritual, and our inordinate attachment to things carnal and temporal. Forgive, we beseech thee, our unkind-ness to one another. Forgive us that in honour we have sought our own selves first and not others; that we have not borne one another's burdens. Open the way of the future for us, that we may walk without stumbling, that we may live with a higher purpose and better accompl-ishment; that we may not only be forgiven for past sin, but be cured of those infirmities out of which so many of our transgressions spring. Amen.

Henry Ward Beecher, 1813-1887

In the evening

Cleanse me by thine own incoming and keep me pure by thine own indwelling. Deliver me from all unworthy bondage; set me free from everything that hampers my usefulness and interrupts my service.

Walter James, 1879-1908

Forgive me my sins, O Lord—the sins of my present and the sins of my past, the sins of my soul and the sins of my body, the sins which I have done to please myself and the sins which I have done to please others. Forgive me the sins, which I have laboured so to hide, that I have hidden them even from myself. O Lord, forgive them all; for Jesus Christ's sake.

Thomas Wilson, 1663-1755

Him that cometh unto me I will in no wise cast out.
(John 6:37)

Jesus calls us; o'er the tumult
    Of our life's wild restless sea,
Day by day his voice is sounding,
    Saying, 'Christian, follow me';

In our joys and in our sorrows,
    Days of toil and hours of ease,
Still he calls, in cares and pleasures,
    'Christian, love me more than these'.

Cecil F Alexander, 1818-1895

Daily Reading
Isaiah 55 (selected) and Matthew 11:28-30

Ho, every one that thirsteth, come ye to the waters, and he that hath no money; come ye, buy, and eat; yea, come, buy wine and milk without money and without price.

Wherefore do ye spend money for that which is not bread? and your labour for that which satisfieth not?

Seek ye the Lord while he may be found, call ye upon him while he is near:

Let the wicked forsake his way, and the unrighteous man his thoughts: and let him return unto the Lord, and he will have mercy upon him; and to our God, for he will abundantly pardon.

Jesus said, Come unto me, all ye that labour and are heavy laden, and I will give you rest.

Take my yoke upon you, and learn of me; for I am meek and lowly in heart: and ye shall find rest unto your souls.

Prayers
In the morning

Warm our cold hearts, Lord, we beseech thee. Take away all that hinders us from giving ourselves to thee. Mould us according to thine own image. Give us grace to obey thee in all things, and ever to follow thy gracious leading. Make us this day to be kind to our fellow men, to be gentle and unselfish; careful to hurt no one by word or deed, but anxious to do good to all, and to make others happy. Keep us from sin this day; for Jesus Christ's sake. Amen.

Bishop Ashton Oxenden, 1808-1892

In the evening

O Lord, my God, give to my heart to long for thee; longing to seek; seeking to find; finding to love; loving to redeem my evils. Give, O Lord my God, to my heart penitence; to my spirit contrition; to my eyes tears for my sins; to my hands the touch of compassion for men. Extinguish in me the desires of the flesh, and kindle in me the fires of thy love. Drive forth from me the spirit of pride and graciously give me the spirit of thy humility. Remove from me the madness of anger, and bestow on me the shield of patience. Keep me from rancour of mind, and in thy gentleness grant me sweetness of disposition. Give me, O most merciful Father, firm faith, befitting hope, and increasing charity. Amen.

Anselm, 1033-1109 (adapted)

THIRTEENTH DAY

The Lord is my helper. (Hebrew 13:6)

> Father of heaven, whose love profound,
> A ransom for our souls have found,
> Before thy throne we sinners bend:
> To us thy pardoning love extend.
> Eternal spirit, by whose breath
> The soul is raised from sin and death,
> Before thy throne we sinners bend:
> To us thy quickening power extend.

Edward Cooper, 1770-1833

Daily Reading
Psalm 18 (selected)

I will love thee, O Lord, my strength.

The Lord is my rock, and my fortress, and my deliverer; my God, my strength, in whom I will trust; my buckler, the horn of my salvation, and my high tower.

I will call upon the Lord, who is worthy to be praised.

The sorrows of hell compassed me about; the fear of death struck terror into my soul.

In my distress I called upon the Lord, and

cried unto my God: he heard my voice, and my cry came before him, even into his ears.

He sent from above, he took me, he drew me out of many waters.

As for God, his way is perfect: the word of the Lord is tried: he is a buckler to all those that trust in him.

Prayers
In the morning
Almighty God, of thy mercy heal us of those things that mar the beauty of life. From all meanness and lying, from all falseness and fear, good Lord deliver us. From ignorance, from stupidity, from blindness of thy glorious works, O Lord deliver us. Open our eyes to behold thy beauty; quicken our ears to hear thy voice; unloose our tongues to sing thy praises; strengthen our hands to do thy work; touch our hearts that we may feel compassion for others; expand our minds that we may know thee, and let the beauty of the Lord our God be upon us; through Jesus Christ our Lord. Amen.

George Dawson, 1821-1876 (adapted)

In the evening
O God, whose never-failing providence ordereth all things both in heaven and earth; we humbly beseech thee to put away from us all hurtful things, and to give us those things which are profitable for us; through Jesus Christ our Lord. Amen.

Gelasian Sacramentary, 494

O Lord to whom all hearts are open, thou canst govern the vessel of our soul far better than we can. Arise, O Lord, and command the strong wind and the troubled sea of our hearts to be still, and at peace in thee. Let thy Holy Spirit dwell in us continually; fill us with divine love, with devout and heavenly thoughts, with comfort and strength, with joy and peace. Amen.

Johann Arndt, 1555-1621

FOURTEENTH DAY

Have faith in God. (Mark 11:22)
Be not afraid, only believe. (Mark 5:36)

A noble army, men and boys,
　　The matron and the maid,
Around the Saviour's throne rejoice,
　　In robes of light arrayed:
They climbed the steep ascent of heaven,
　　Through peril, toil and pain;
O God, to us may grace be given
　　To follow in their train.

Reginald Heber, 1783-1826

Daily Reading
Hebrews 11 (selected) and 12:1-3
Now faith is the substance of things hoped for, the evidence of things not seen.

It was because of their faith that the men of old stand on record.

It is faith that lets us understand how the universe was fashioned by the Word of God, so that the visible came forth from the invisible.

Why then, with all these witnesses to faith around us, we must throw off every encumbrance, every sin to which we cling, and run with resolution the race for which we are entered, our eyes fixed on Jesus, on whom faith depends from start to finish. Take your standard from him, and you will not grow faint, you will not find your soul unmanned.

Prayers

In the morning

O my Father, I have moments of deep unrest —moments when I know not what to ask by reason of the very excess of my wants. I have in these hours no words for thee. My cry seems purely worldly. Yet all the time thou hast accepted my unrest as a prayer, as a cry to thee. I know not what to ask, but thou knowest the need which lies beneath my speechless groan. Thou knowest that, because I am made in thine image, I can find rest only in thee. Hear, therefore, the wordless cry of my heart and out of thy abundant mercy supply all my need. Amen.

George Matheson, 1842-1906 (adapted)

In the evening

Lord increase our faith, that feeling towards thee as children, we may trust where we cannot see, and hope where all seems doubtful, ever looking unto thee as our Father who ordereth all things well. Amen.

George Dawson, 1821-1876

O Lord, teach us so to number our days that we may apply our hearts unto wisdom. Lighten, if it be thy will, the pressure of this world's cares, and above all reconcile us to thy will, and give us a peace which the world cannot take away; through Jesus Christ our Lord. Amen

Thomas Chalmers, 1780-1847

FIFTEENTH DAY

Incline thine ear unto wisdom, and apply thy heart to understanding. If thou seek her as silver, and search for her as for hid treasures; then shalt thou become aware of the power and presence of the Lord, and find the knowledge of God.
(Proverbs 2:2, 3 and 5)

Lead us, heavenly Father, lead us
    O'er the world's tempestuous sea;
Guard us, guide us, keep us, feed us,
    For we have no help but thee,
Yet possessing ever blessing,
    If our God our Father be.

James Edmeston, 1791-1867

Daily Reading
Psalm 73 (selected)

First uncertainty:

But as for me, my feet were almost gone;
My steps had well nigh slipped.
For I was envious at the arrogant,
When I saw the prosperity of the wicked.

Then vision:

When I thought how I might know this,
It was too painful for me;
Until I went into the sanctuary of God,
And considered their latter end.

Then, positive assurance:

Whom have I in heaven but thee?
And there is none on earth that I desire
    beside thee.
My flesh and my heart faileth;
But God is the strength of my heart and my
    portion for ever.

Prayers
In the morning

O thou, who hast said, 'Learn of me, for I am meek and lowly of heart,' grant unto us the spirit of humility.

Free us from the cowardice that is afraid to face new truth;

Deliver us from the laziness that is content with half-truths;

Above all, keep us from the arrogance that thinks it knows all truth.

Amen.

Thomas a Kempis, 1379-1471

Lord, who knowest all things, and lovest all men, thine is the might, and wisdom, and love to save us.

From all perplexity of mind; from loneliness of thought, and discontented brooding, and especially from whatever sin besets us, save and deliver us, O Lord.

Rowland Williams, 1818-1870

In the evening

O gracious and compassionate Father, look on us in mercy and to all sorrowing hearts be thou a very present Help and Refuge. Reveal to us thy mighty Presence in all the circumstances of our lot. Be thou the comfort of our hearts when they mourn and are dismayed; speak gently to us when we are overwhelmed with sorrow, and fear presses hard upon us.

Purify our hearts and minds through the holy fire of thy Cross, and the harder our trials, the nearer be thou, O God, with thy comfort and strength. Amen.

Gottfried Arnold, 1665-1714

SIXTEENTH DAY

Teach me thy way, O Lord, and lead me in a plain path. (Psalm 27:11)

Lead us, O Father, in the paths of peace:
　　Without thy guiding hand we go astray,

And doubts appal, and sorrows still increase;
   Lead us through Christ, the true and living way.

Lead us, O Father, in the paths of right:
   Blindly we stumble when we walk alone,
Involved in shadows of a darkening night;
   Only with thee we journey safely on.

W H Burleigh, 1812-1871

Daily Reading
James I (selected) and Proverbs 3 (selected)
Every good gift and every perfect gift is from
above, and cometh down from the Father of
light, with whom is no variableness, neither
shadow of turning.

If any of you lack wisdom, let him ask of
God, who giveth to all men liberally, and it shall
be given him. But let him ask in faith nothing
wavering.

Trust in the Lord with all thine heart; and
lean not unto thine own understanding.

In all thy ways acknowledge him, and he
shall direct thy paths.

Then shalt thou walk in thy way safely, and
thy foot shall not stumble.

The path of the just is as the shining light, that
shineth more and more unto the perfect day.

Prayers
In the morning

O Heavenly Father, in whom we live and move
and have our being, we humbly pray thee so to

35

guide and govern us by thy Holy Spirit, that in all the cares and occupations of this day we may never forget thee, but remember we are ever walking in thy sight; for thine own Name's sake. Amen.

Ancient Collect, 440

O Lord our God, teach us to ask thee for the right blessings. Steer thou the vessel of our life towards thyself. Show us the course wherein we should go. Let thy Spirit curb our wayward senses. Guide and enable us to keep thy laws and in all our work evermore to rejoice in thy glorious and gladdening Presence.

St Basil, 379

In the evening
We beseech thee, O Lord, let the power of thy Holy Spirit be present with us, that he may both mercifully cleanse our hearts, and protect us from all adversities; through Jesus Christ our Lord. Amen.

Leonine Sacramentary, 440

O God, who seest all our weaknesses and the troubles we labour under, have regard to the prayers of thy servant who stands in need of thy comfort, thy direction, and thy help. Thou alone knowest what is best for us; let me never dispute thy wisdom or thy goodness. Grant that I may never murmur at thy Appointments, but prepare my heart and give me strength that no affliction may overbear me. Amen.

Thomas Wilson, 1663-1755 (adapted)

SEVENTEENTH DAY

They that wait upon the Lord shall renew their strength. (Isaiah 40:31)

Father, hear the prayer we offer:
   Not for ease thy prayer shall be,
But for strength, that we may ever
   Live our lives courageously.

Be our strength in times of weakness,
   In our wanderings be our guide;
Through endeavour, failure, danger,
   Father, be thou at our side.

L Maria Willis 1824-1908

Daily Reading
2 Corinthians 12 *(selected)*

It is not expedient for me doubtless to boast.

And lest I should be exalted above measure through the abundance of the revelations, there was given to me a thorn in the flesh which came as Satan's messenger to bruise me.

Three times I begged the Lord to rid me of it,

but his answer was: 'My grace is sufficient for thee: for my strength is made perfect in weakness'. I shall therefore prefer to find my joy and pride in the very things that are my weakness, that the power of Christ may rest upon me.

Hence I am well content, for Christ's sake, with weakness, contempt, persecution, hardship, and frustration; for when I am weak, then am I strong.

Prayers
In the morning
O God, from whom we have received life and all earthly blessings, give unto us this day what we need. Give unto all of us strength to perform faithfully our appointed tasks; bless the work of our hands and of our minds. Grant that we may ever serve thee, in sickness and in health, in necessity and in abundance; sanctify our joys and our trials, and give us grace to seek first thy Kingdom and its righteousness, in the sure and certain faith that all else shall be added unto us; through Jesus Christ, thy Son, our Lord and Saviour. Amen.

Eugene Bersier, 1831-1887

In the evening
O God, our Maker and Friend, who dwellest with us, and dost uphold us so that we are not alone; comfort us always with the conviction of thy presence, and help us when the way is weary, and the burden is heavy, and the task is hard, to lean ourselves for spirit and strength

upon the thought of thee. We come to thee in prayer, feeling our need of some stronger, deeper inspiration for the trials of life; of some stronger, deeper inspiration to assist us in bearing them. Show us for our help thy glory. Amen.

S A Tipple, 1828-1912

EIGHTEENTH DAY

Thou canst make me clean. (Matthew 8:2)

> Rock of ages, cleft for me,
> Let me hide myself in thee;
> Let the water and the blood,
> From thy riven side which flowed,
> Be of sin the doubtful cure;
> Cleanse me from its guilt and power.

A M Toplady, 1740-1778

Daily Reading
Psalm 51:7-10, Isaiah 1:18,
John 3:16 and 1 John 1:5-9

Hide thy face from my sins, and blot out all my iniquities.

Create in me a clean heart, O God; and renew a right spirit within me.

Come now, and let us reason together, saith the Lord: though your sins be as scarlet, they shall be as white as snow; though they be red like crimson, they shall be as wool.

God is light, and in him is no darkness at all.

If we walk in the light, as he is in the light, we have fellowship one with another, and the blood of Jesus Christ his Son cleanses us from all sin.

If we confess our sins, he is faithful and just to forgive us our sins, and all our wrong-doing is purged away.

For God so loved the world, that he gave his only begotten Son, that whosoever believeth in him should not perish, but have everlasting life.

Prayers
In the morning

Almighty and Everlasting God, with whom nothing is obscure, nothing dark, send forth thy light into our hearts this day, that we may perceive thy law for us and walking in thy way, may fall into no sin; through thy beloved Son and our beloved example, Jesus Christ. Amen.

St Gregory, 550-604

O God of Love, who art the true sun of the world, evermore risen and never going down, we beseech thee mercifully to shine into our hearts, that the night of sin and the mists of error being driven away, and thou brightly shining within us, we may all our life long go without stumbling in the road which thou hast prepared for us to walk in; through thy Son our Saviour, Christ the Lord. Amen.

Erasmus, 1466-1536

In the evening

O Lord our God, we entreat thy mercy with our whole heart, that, as thou defendest us against things adverse to the body, so thou wilt set us free from the enemies of the soul; and as thou grantest us to rejoice in outward tranquillity, so vouchsafe to us thine inward peace; through Jesus Christ our Lord. Amen.

Leonine Sacramentary, 440

NINETEENTH DAY

If God be for us, who can be against us?
(Romans 8:31)

Fight the good fight with all thy might;
Christ is thy strength, and Christ thy right.
Lay hold on life, and it shall be
Thy joy and crown eternally.

Cast care aside; lean on thy Guide.
His boundless mercy shall provide;
Trust, and thy trusting soul will prove
Christ is its life, and Christ its love.

Faint not, nor fear; his arm is near;
He changeth not, and thou art dear;
Only believe, and thou shalt see
That Christ is all in all to thee.

J S B Monsell, 1811-1875

Daily Reading
Psalm 25 and 118 (selected)

Mine eyes are ever toward the Lord; for he shall pluck my feet out of the net.

Turn thee unto me, and have mercy upon me; for I am desolate and afflicted. The troubles of my heart are enlarged: O bring me out of my distresses. O keep my soul, and deliver me: let me not be ashamed; for I put my trust in thee.

I called upon the Lord in distress: the Lord answered me, and set me in a large place.

The Lord is my strength and song, and is become my salvation.

O give thanks unto the Lord; for he is good: for his mercy endureth for ever.

Prayers
In the morning

Merciful God, who givest us more than we ask or think, do unto us this day according to thy mercy and goodness. Give health to the sick, rest the weary and heavy-laden, comfort the mourner; uphold them that are tempted; raise up them that fall; pardon and restore the penitent; and make us all such as thou wouldst have us to be; through Jesus Christ our Lord. Amen.

Canon E Hawkins, 1802-1868

Go forth into the world in peace; be of good courage; hold fast that which is good; render to no man evil for evil; strengthen the faint-hearted; support the weak; help the afflicted;

honour all men; love and serve the Lord;
rejoicing in the power of the Holy Spirit. Amen.

Revised Prayer Book, 1928

In the evening
O God, who makest all things work together for
good to them that love thee, pour into our
hearts such steadfast love to thee, that those
desires which spring from thee may not be
turned aside by any temptation. Amen.

Roman Breviary

Be present, O merciful God, and protect us
through the silent hours of this night, that we
who are fatigued by the changes and chances of
this fleeting world may repose on thy eternal
changelessness; through Jesus Christ, the same
yesterday, today and forever. Amen.

Leonine Sacramentary, 440

TWENTIETH DAY

Teach me to do thy will. (Psalm 143:10)

My God and Father, while I stray,
Far from my home in life's rough way,
O teach me from my heart to say,
'Thy will be done'.

Though dark my path and sad my lot,
Let me be still and murmur not,
Or breathe the prayer divinely taught,
'Thy will be done'.

Renew my will from day to day:
Blend it with thine, and take away
All that now makes it hard to say,
'Thy will be done'.

Charlotte Elliott, 1789-1871

Daily Reading
Matthew 26 (selected)

Then came Jesus to a place called Gethsemane and said to the disciples, Sit ye here, while I go and pray yonder.

Then he said to them, My heart is sad, sad even to death; stay here and watch with me. Then he went forward a little and fell on his face and prayed, saying, O my Father, if it be possible, let this cup pass from me: nevertheless not as I will but what thou wilt.

Then he went to the disciples and found them asleep; and he said to Peter, What, could you not watch with me for even an hour? Watch and pray, that you may not enter into temptation; the spirit is willing enough but the flesh is weak.

Then he went away again and prayed saying, O my Father, if this cup may not pass away from me, except I drink it, then thy will be done.

Prayers
In the morning

Heavenly Father, who watchest over thy faithful people and mightily defendest them, we thank thee that it has pleased thee to take care of us, thy servants, during the night past, and to give us needful sleep to refresh our bodies. We beseech thee to show the same goodness to us this day, so preserving and ruling over us, that we may neither think or speak nor do anything displeasing to thee or hurtful to ourselves, but that all our doings may be agreeable to thy most holy will. Amen.

Thomas Becon, 1511-1570

In the evening

O Lord, we beseech thee mercifully to receive the prayers of thy people who call upon thee; and grant that they may both perceive and know what things they ought to do, and also may have grace and power faithfully to fulfil the same; through Jesus Christ our Lord. Amen.

Gregorian Sacramentary, 590

Enable us, gracious Father, to pray with sincerity that thy will be done. Keep us from rebellion and bitter thoughts. Let us not become dejected or impatient under any of the troubles of this life, but ever find rest and comfort in the thought, 'This is the will of my Father and my

God, and we believe thou doest all things well';
grant this for Jesus Christ's sake. Amen.

Thomas Wilson, 1663-1755 (adapted)

TWENTY-FIRST DAY

God shall supply all your need. (Philippians 4:19)

I waited for the Lord my God,
  And patiently did bear;
At length to me he did incline,
  My voice and cry to hear.

He took me from a fearful pit
  And from the miry clay,
And on a rock he set my feet,
  Establishing my way.

Francis Rous, 1579-1659
and W Barton, 1597-1678

Daily Reading
Psalm 69 (selected)

Save me, O God, for the waters are come in unto
my soul.
  I sink in deep mire, where there is no standing.
  I am come into deep waters, where the floods
overflow me.
  I am weary of my crying; my throat is dried:
mine eyes fail while I wait for my God.

O God, thou knowest my foolishness; and my sins are not hid from thee.

O God in the multitude of thy mercy hear me.

Deliver me out of the mire, and let me not sink.

Let not the waterflood overflow me, neither let the deep swallow me up, and let not the pit shut her mouth upon me.

Hear me, O Lord: turn unto me according to the multitude of thy tender mercies, and hide not thy face from thy servant; for I am in trouble: hear me speedily.

Prayers
In the morning

Into thy hands, O Lord, we commit ourselves this day. Give to each one of us a watchful, a humble, and a diligent spirit, that we may seek in all things to know thy will, and when we know it may perform it perfectly and gladly, to the honour and glory of thy name; through Jesus Christ our Lord. Amen.

Gelasian Sacramentary, 494

May the hand of God ever keep us. May the grace of Christ continually defend us from all evil. O Lord, direct our heart in the way of peace; through Jesus Christ our Lord. Amen.

Prayer Book of Aedelwald

In the evening

Almighty God, our Heavenly Father, who lovest all and forgettest none, we bring to thee our supplications for all thy children.

We remember before thee those who are sick in body and in mind. All who have been bereaved, all who are troubled by suffering or sin. We pray for all who are absorbed in their own grief, that they may be raised to share the sorrows of others, and thus know the blessed fellowship of the Cross. For all who are lonely and sad we pray that they may know thee as their Friend and Comforter. Remember, O Lord, the aged and infirm, all who are growing weary with the journey of life, all who are passing through the valley of shadows, that they may find the risen Christ is with them and that there is light at evening time. Amen.

Dr John Hunter, 1849-1917

TWENTY-SECOND DAY

There is a friend that sticketh closer than a brother. (Proverbs 18:24)

What a friend we have in Jesus,
    All our sins and griefs to bear!
What a privilege to carry
    Everything to God in prayer!

O what peace we often forfeit,
    O what needless pain we bear—
All because we do not carry
    Everything to God in prayer.

Joseph Scriven, 1819-1886

Daily Reading
John 15 and 17 (selected)

As the Father hath loved me, so have I loved you: continue ye in my love.

If ye keep my commandments, ye shall abide in my love: even as I have kept my Father's commandments, and abide in his love;

These things have I spoken unto you, that my joy might remain in you, and that your joy might be full.

This is my commandment, that ye love one another, as I have loved you.

Greater love hath no man than this, that a man lay down his life for his friends.

Ye are my friends, if you do whatsoever I command you.

These things I command you, that ye love one another. That you all may be one as my Father and I are one, and that the love wherewith my Father has loved me may be in you.

Prayers
In the morning

Be mindful this day, O God, of all who stand in need of thy great tenderness of heart, for thou art the help of the helpless, the hope of the hopeless, the Saviour of the tempest-tossed, the haven of those who sail life's troubled sea, and the God and Father of our Lord Jesus Christ. Amen.

Coptic Liturgy of St Basil, fourth century

Almighty and most merciful Father, who hast given us a new commandment that we should love one another, give us also the grace that we may fulfil it. Make us gentle, courteous, and forebearing. Direct our lives so that we may look each to the good of others in word and deed. Hallow all our friendships by the blessing of thy Spirit, for his sake who loved us and gave himself for us, Jesus Christ our Lord. Amen.

Bishop Westcott, 1825-1901

In the evening

O Lord, our heavenly Father, by whose Divine ordinance the darkness covers the earth and brings unto us bodily rest and quietness, we render thee our grateful thanks for the loving-kindness which thou hast shown in preserving us during the past day, and in giving us all things necessary for our health and comfort. And we beseech thee, for Jesus Christ's sake, to forgive us all sins we have committed in thougt, word, or deed, and that thou wilt shadow us this night under the wings of thy almighty power, and defend us from all powers of evil. Amen.

Thomas Becon, 1511-1570

TWENTY-THIRD DAY

The people that walked in darkness have seen a great light: they that dwell in the land of the shadow of death, upon them hath the light shined. (Isaiah 9:2)

Thou whose almighty word
Chaos and darkness heard
   And took their flight,
Hear us, we humbly pray,
And where the gospel day
Sheds not its glorious ray,
   Let there be light.

Thou who didst come to bring
On thy redeeming wing
   Healing and sight,
Health to the sick mind,
Sight to the inly blind,
O now to all mankind
   Let there be light.

John Marriott, 1780-1825

Daily Reading
Psalm 130

Out of the depths have I cried unto thee, O Lord.

Lord, hear my voice; let thine ears be attentive to the voice of my supplications.

If thou, Lord, shouldest mark inquities, O Lord, who shall stand?

But there is forgiveness with thee, that thou mayest be feared.

I wait for the Lord, my soul doth wait, and in his word do I hope.

Hope in the Lord: for with the Lord there is mercy, and with him is plenteous redemption.

Prayers
In the morning
We give thee grateful thanks for the rest of the past night and for the gift of a new day with its opportunities of pleasing thee. Grant that we may so pass its hours in the perfect freedom of thy service, that at eventide we may again give thanks unto thee; through Jesus Christ our Lord. Amen.

Daybreak Office of the Eastern Church,
third century

O Lord, thou knowest how busy we must be this day; if we forget thee, do not thou forget us; for Christ's sake. Amen.

General Lord Astley, 1579-1652
Prayer before the Battle of Edgehill, 1642

O God, I thank thee for all the joy I have had in life. Amen.

Earl Brihtnoth, 991

In the evening
O Christ our Lord, who art the greatest Physician, grant unto all who are sick the aid of heavenly healing, and vouchsafe to deliver them from all sickness and infirmity; through Jesus Christ. Amen.

Mozarabic Liturgy, c. 600

O Lord Jesus Christ, who art the Way, the Truth, and the Life, we pray thee suffer us not to stray from thee, who art the Way, nor to distrust thee, who art the Truth, nor to rest in any other thing than thee, who art the Life. Teach us by thy Holy Spirit what to believe, what to do, and wherein to take our rest. For thine own name's sake we ask it. Amen.

Erasmus, 1466-1536

TWENTY-FOURTH DAY

Praise and extol and honour the King of Heaven. (Daniel 4:37)

Praise my soul, the King of Heaven;
    To his feet thy tribute bring;
Ransomed, healed, restored, forgiven,
    Who like me his praise should sing?
Praise him, praise him, praise him, praise him,
    Praise the everlasting King.

Father-like he tends and spares us;
    Well our feeble frame he knows;
In his hands he gently bears us,
    Rescues us from all his foes;
Praise him, praise him, praise him, praise him,
    Widely as his mercy flows.

H Lyte, 1793-1847

Daily Reading
Psalm 84 (selected)

How amiable are thy tabernacles, O Lord of hosts!

My soul longeth, yea, even fainteth for the courts of the Lord: my heart and my flesh cry out for the living God.

Yea, the sparrow hath found an house, and the swallow a nest for herself, where she may lay her young, even thine altars, O Lord of hosts, my King, and my God.

Blessed are they that dwell in thy house.

Blessed is the man whose strength is in thee.

For the Lord God is a sun and shield: no good thing will he withhold from them that trust in him.

They go from strength to strength.

O Lord of hosts, blessed is the man that trusteth in thee.

Prayers
In the morning

O Lord, move us by thine example to show kindness and do good to others this day. Grant us patience and forbearance with all sufferers, gracious or ungracious, grateful or ungrateful, that in our stumbling walk and scant measure, they may yet discern in us a vestige of thee, and give thee the glory.

Christina G Rossetti, 1830-1895

We thank thee for every inspiring thought with which we have been comforted and strengthened; for every helpful friend we have found;

for such high aims as we have learned to cherish, and are still pursuing, albeit sometimes with lame feet; we thank thee for all uplifting ministries we find in social converse, in books, pictures, music, in poets' dreams, in facts and marvels of science and for all clean laughter. For these and all thy gifts we thank thee; through Jesus Christ our Lord. Amen.

S A Tipple, 1828-1912 (adapted)

In the evening
Our God and our Father, we need peace. We would receive from thee the peace that passeth understanding, which the world cannot give and cannot take away. We need love. Flood us with thy love; cleanse us of the resentful vindictiveness and unbrotherliness which infest our lives. Make us kind; give us a spirit of understanding, tolerance for all sorts and conditions of men. Take meanness from us, fill us with thyself. We need power. The eternal treasures of thy strength are at our disposal, grant that we may be strengthened with the might of thy spirit in the inner man. Amen.

Author unknown

TWENTY-FIFTH DAY

Let every man take heed how he builds his life. There can be no other secure foundation beyond that which is already laid, which is Jesus Christ himself.
(1 Corinthians 3:10-11, adapted).

He only is my Rock and my Salvation.
(Psalm 62:2)

> City of God, how broad and far
>   Outspread thy walls sublime!
> The true thy chartered freemen are,
>   Of every age and clime.
>
> In vain the surge's angry shock,
>   In vain the drifting sands;
> Unharmed upon the eternal Rock
>   The eternal City stands.

Samuel Johnson, 1822-1882

Daily Reading
Matthew 7:24-27

The point of this story is that a testing time comes to each one of us, and it depends on what foundation we have built our life whether it stands life's strain and stress or collapses about us in ruins.

Therefore, said Jesus, whosoever heareth these sayings of mine, and doeth them, I will liken him unto a wise man, who built his house upon a rock. And the rain descended, and the floods came, and the winds blew, and beat upon that house; and it fell not; for it was founded upon a rock.

And everyone that heareth these sayings of mine, and doeth them not, shall be likened unto a foolish man, who built his house upon the sand. And the rain descended, and floods came, and the winds blew, and beat upon that house; and it fell: and great was the fall of it.

Prayers

In the morning

O Lord God, may it please thee this day to order and to hallow, to rule and to govern our hearts and our bodies, our thoughts, our words, and our actions; through Jesus Christ our Lord. Amen.

Roman Breviary

Be present, O Lord, and protect us by day as well as by night, that in all successive changes of time we may be ever strengthened by thine unchangeableness; through Jesus Christ our Lord. Amen.

Leonine Sacramentary, 440

Grant to us, O Lord, to know that which is worth knowing; to love that which is worth loving; to praise that which can bear with praise; to hate what in thy sight is unworthy; to prize what to thee is precious, and above all to search out and to do what is well-pleasing unto thee; through Jesus Christ our Lord. Amen.

Thomas a Kempis, 1379-1471

In the evening

O God, from whom to turn away is to fall, in whom to abide is to stand for ever, teach us how to know thee, and build us to be temples worthy of thy glory; through Jesus Christ our Lord. Amen.

St Augustine, 354-430

May the strength of God pilot us.
May the power of God preserve us.
May the wisdom of God instruct us.
May the hand of God protect us.
May the way of God direct us.
May the shield of God defend us.

St Patrick, 373

TWENTY-SIXTH DAY

Lead us not into temptation. (Matthew 6:13)

Yield not to temptation, for yielding is sin,
Each victory will help you some other to win;
Fight manfully onward, dark passions subdue,
Look ever to Jesus, he will carry you through.
To him that o'ercometh God giveth a crown.
Through faith we shall conquer, though often
cast down;
He who is our Saviour our strength will renew,
Look ever to Jesus, he will carry you through.

H R Palmer, 1834-1907

Daily Reading
Matthew 26:41; 1 Corinthians 10:12-14;
Hebrews 2:18 and James 1:12-15

Temptation arises when a man is enticed and lured away by his own lust; then lust conceives and gives birth to sin; and sin full-grown breeds death.

Watch and pray, that ye enter not into temptation: the spirit is indeed willing but the flesh is weak.

Wherefore let him that thinketh he standeth take heed lest he fall.

There hath no temptation taken you but such as is common to man: but God is faithful, who will not suffer you to be tempted above that ye are able; but will with the temptation also make a way to escape, that ye may be able to bear it.

For in that he himself hath suffered being tempted, he is able to succour them that are tempted.

Blessed is the man who remains steadfast under temptation, for having passed that test he will win that crown of life, which God has promised to those who love him.

Prayers
In the morning

O Lord our heavenly Father, Almighty and Ever-lasting God, who hast safely brought us to the beginning of this day; defend us in the same with thy mighty power, and grant that this day we fall into no sin, neither run into any kind of danger; but that all our doings may be ordered by thy governance, to do always that which is righteous in thy sight; through Jesus Christ our Lord. Amen.

Gelasian Sacramentary, 494

Almighty God, in whom is no darkness at all, grant us thy light perpetually, and when we cannot see the way before us, may we continue to put our trust in thee, that so being guided and guarded, we may be kept from falling this day, and finally by thy mercy, enter into our rest; through Jesus Christ our Lord. Amen.

William A Knight, 1836-1916

In the evening

O God of Love, who hast given us a commandment that we should love one another, even as thou didst love us and give thy beloved Son for our salvation; we pray thee to give to us a mind forgetful of past ill-will and a heart to love our brethren for the sake of Jesus Christ, our Lord and only Saviour. Amen.

Coptic, Liturgy of St Cyril, fifth century

O Lord Jesus, because, being full of foolishness, we often sin and have to ask pardon, help us to forgive as we would be forgiven, neither mentioning old offences committed against us, nor dwelling upon them in thought, nor being influenced by them in heart; but loving each other freely, as thou freely lovest us; for thy name's sake. Amen.

Christina G Rossetti, 1830-1894

TWENTY-SEVENTH DAY

Whereby are given unto us exceeding great and precious promises. (2 Peter 1:4)

O Word of God incarnate,
O Wisdom from on high,
O Truth unchanged, unchanging,
O Light of our dark sky,
We praise thee for the radiance
That from the hallowed page,
A lantern to our footsteps,
Shines on from age to age.

W W How, 1823-1897

Daily Reading
The Beatitudes (paraphrased)
and Matthew 5:3-9

Blessed is the man who, because he has no earthly resources, puts his whole trust in God. He is a citizen of the kingdom of heaven.

Blessed are those who suffer pain or loss, for that is how we become strong. They will find consolation and the joy of God.

Those who are humble and willing to take a lowly place are happy for they will be honoured by God.

Those who seek and strive to put wrong things right will be satisfied for that is exactly what God is doing.

People who are ready to forgive others will find themselves kindly judged.

Those who are sincere and pure in heart will come to a knowledge of God's purpose for themselves and the world and one day will see God.

Those who seek to bring people together in understanding and friendship are happy for they are doing God's will.

Prayers
In the morning
O Lord Jesus Christ, give us a measure of thy Spirit, that we may be enabled to obey thy teaching, to pacify anger, to take part in pity, to moderate desire, to increase love, to put away sorrow, to cast away vain glory, nor to be vindictive, nor to fear death, ever entrusting our spirit to immortal God, who with thee and the Holy Ghost liveth and reigneth world without end. Amen.

Apollonius, c. 185

This prayer was made by Apollonius during his trial before the Roman Prefect, Terentius, who gave judgement as follows: 'I would fain let thee go; but I cannot because of the decree of the Senate'. So Apollonius was executed.

In the evening
O thou God of Peace, unite our hearts by thy bond of peace, that we may live with one another continually in peace and unity.

O thou God of Patience, give us patience in the time of trial, and steadfastness to endure to the end.

O thou gentle Wind of the Holy Spirit, cool and refresh our hearts in all heat and anguish. Be our Defence and Shade in time of need, our Help in trial, our Consolation when all things are against us.

Come, O thou eternal Light, Salvation and Comfort, be our Light in darkness, our Salvation in life, our Comfort in death; and lead us in the straight way to everlasting life, that we may praise thee forever. Amen.

Bernhard Albrecht, 1569-1636

TWENTY-EIGHTH DAY

What shall I render unto the Lord for all his benefits? (Psalm 116:12)

God be in my head, and in my understanding;
God be in mine eyes, and in my looking;
God be in my mouth, and in my speaking;
God be in my heart, and in my thinking;
God be at mine end, and at my departing.

Book of Hours, 1514

Daily Reading
Mark 12:28-34

There are two things the human heart needs and craves:

   (1) Someone to love and worship—the Lord thy God.

   (2) Someone to love and work for—your neighbour as yourself.

   And one of the scribes asked him, Which is the first commandment of all?

   And Jesus answered him, The first of all the commandments is, Hear, O Israel; The Lord our God is one Lord; And thou shalt love the Lord thy God with all thy heart, and with all thy soul, and with all thy mind, and with all thy strength:

this is the first commandment. And the second is like, namely this, Thou shalt love thy neighbour as thyself. There is none other commandment greater than these.

And the scribe said unto him, Well, Master, thou hast said the truth: for there is one God; and there is none other but he: and to love him with all the heart, and with all the understanding, and with all the soul, and with all the strength, and to love his neighbour as himself, is more than whole burnt-offerings and sacrifices.

Prayers
In the morning

O thou most holy and ever-loving God, we thank thee once more for the quiet rest of the night that has gone by, for the new promise that has come with this fresh morning, and for the hope of this day. While we have slept, the world in which we live has swept on as we have rested under the shadow of thy love. May we trust thee this day for all the needs of the body, the soul and the spirit. Amen.

Robert Collyer, 1823-1912

In the evening

O Lord our God, refresh us with quiet sleep when we are wearied with the day's labour, that, being assisted with the help our weakness needs, we may be devoted to thee both in body and mind; through Jesus Christ our Lord. Amen

Leonine Sacramentary, 440

O God, who through the grace of thy Holy Spirit, dost pour the gift of love into the hearts of thy faithful people, grant unto us health, both of mind and body, that we may love thee with our whole strength. Grant us grace to be kindly affectioned one to another with brotherly love; in honour preferring one another; and that we may always do those things which are pleasing unto thee; through Jesus Christ our Lord. Amen.

Sarum Breviary, 1085 (adapted)

TWENTY-NINTH DAY

That your joy may be full. (John 16:24)

> All things praise thee, Lord most high,
> Heaven and earth and sea and sky,
> All were for thy glory made,
> That thy greatness, thus displayed,
> Should all worship bring to thee;
> All things praise thee: Lord, may we.
>
> All things praise thee: gracious Lord,
> Great Creator, powerful Word,
> Omnipresent Spirit, now
> At thy feet we humbly bow,
> Lift our hearts in praise to thee;
> All things praise thee: Lord, may we.

G W Conder, 1821-1874

Daily Reading
Psalm 95:1-7 and 98:1

O come let us sing unto the Lord; let us make a joyful noise to the rock of our salvation.

Let us come before his presence with thanksgiving, and make a joyful noise unto him with psalms.

For the Lord is a great God, and a great King, above all gods.

In his hand are the deep places of the earth: the strength of the hills is his also. The sea is his, and he made it: and his hands formed the dry land.

O come, let us worship and bow down: let us kneel before the Lord our maker. For he is our God; and we are the people of his pasture, and the sheep of his hand.

O sing unto the Lord a new song for he hath done marvellous things.

Prayers
In the morning
Te Deum Laudamus

We praise thee, O God; we acknowledge thee to be the Lord.

All the earth doth worship thee, the Father everlasting.

To thee all Angels cry aloud; the Heavens and all the Powers therein.

To thee Cherubin and Seraphin continually do cry,

'Holy, Holy, Holy, Lord God of Sabaoth;

Heaven and earth are full of the Majesty of thy glory'.

The glorious company of the Apostles praise thee.

The goodly fellowship of the Prophets praise thee.

The noble army of Martyrs praise thee.

The holy Church throughout all the world doth acknowledge thee.

Day by day we magnify thee;

And we worship thy Name ever world without end. Amen.

In the evening

O Almighty God, who alone canst order the unruly wills and affections of sinful men; grant unto thy people, that they may love the thing which thou commandest, and desire that which thou dost promise; that so, among the sundry and manifold changes of this world, our hearts may be fixed where true joys are to be found; through Jesus Christ our Lord. Amen.

Gelasian Sacramentary, 494

Heavenly Father, we commit ourselves to thee; take us in thy care this night. Cause us to lie down in peace and to rise in safety; be thou ever near us, and defend us from the terrors of night, that when we wake, whether it be in this life or the next, we may still be with thee. Amen.

Thomas Dee, 1843

THIRTIETH DAY

This is the victory that overcometh the world, even our faith. (1 John 5:4)

> Drop thy still dews of quietness,
>   Till all our strivings cease;
> Take from our souls the strain and stress,
> And let our ordered lives confess
>   The beauty of thy peace.
>
> Breathe through the heats of our desire
>   Thy coolness and thy balm;
> Let sense be dumb, let flesh retire;
> Speak through the earthquake, wind, and fire,
>   O still small voice of calm!

J G Whittier, 1807-1892

Daily Reading
Luke 11:9-13 and John 15:7

I say unto you, Ask, and it shall be given you; seek, and ye shall find; knock and it shall be opened unto you.

For everyone that asketh receiveth; and he that seeketh findeth; and to him that knocketh it shall be opened.

If a son shall ask bread of any of you that is a father, will he give him a stone? or if he ask a fish, will he for a fish give him a serpent? or if he shall ask an egg, will he offer him a scorpion?

If ye then, being evil, know how to give good gifts unto your children; how much more shall your heavenly Father give the Holy Spirit to them that ask him?

If you abide in me, and my words abide in you, ye shall ask what you will, and it shall be done unto you.

Prayers
In the morning

Spirit of purity and grace,
    Our weakness pitying see:
O make our hearts thy dwelling-place,
    And worthier thee.

Harriet Auber, 1773-1862

O Lord, cure our infirmities, pardon our offences, lighten our burdens, enrich our poverty.

Dr Christopher Sutton, 1565-1629

Grant thy servants, O God, to be filled with thy grace, and to go forward by thine aid. Give us a right faith, perfect love, true humility. Grant there may be in us simple affection, brave patience, persevering obedience, perpetual peace, a pure mind, an honest heart and spirit-ual strength; thorough Jesus Christ our Lord. Amen.

Gallican Sacramentary (adapted)

In the evening
Abide with us, Good Lord, this night and for ever. May we lie down with full trust in thy goodness and in perfect charity with all men,

and be raised up again to praise thee for all thy
mercies; through Jesus Christ our Lord. Amen.

Archbishop Benson, 1829-1896

O God, who hast prepared for them that love
thee such good things as pass man's understanding, pour into our hearts such love towards thee, that we, loving thee above all
things, may obtain thy promises, which exceed
all that we can desire; through Jesus Christ our
Lord. Amen.

Gelasian Sacramentary, 494

THIRTY-FIRST DAY

In this will I be confident. (Psalm 27:3)
My Refuge, my Saviour. (2 Samuel 22:3)

Blessed assurance, Jesus is mine;
O what a foretaste of glory divine!
Heir of salvation, purchase of God;
Born of his Spirit, washed in his blood.

Frances (Crosby) van Alstyne, 1820-1915

I am not skilled to understand
What God hath willed, what God hath
    planned;
I only know at his right hand
Stands One who is my Saviour.

Dora Greenwell, 1821-1882

Daily Reading
Psalm 62 (selected) and Jude 1:24-25

Truly my soul waiteth upon God: from him cometh my salvation.

He only is my rock and my salvation; he is my defence; I shall not be greatly moved.

My soul, wait thou only upon God; for my expectation is from him.

In God is my salvation and my glory; the rock of my strength; my refuge is in God.

God is a refuge for us. Trust in him at all times.

Now unto him who is able to keep you from falling, and to present you faultless before the presence of his glory with exceeding joy, to the only wise God our Saviour, be glory and majesty, dominion and power, both now and ever.

Prayers
In the morning

What will befall us today, O God, we know not; we only know that nothing will happen which thou hast not foreseen, determined, desired, and ordered—that is enough for us. Thee do we worship and adore. We ask in the Name of Jesus Christ our Saviour, and through his infinite merits, patience in all our sufferings, perfect submission to thee for all that thou desirest or permittest, guidance in all that we undertake; for thine honour and glory we ask it. Amen.

Princess Elizabeth, 1770-1840

In the evening

O God, our Lord, the stay of all them that put their trust in thee, wherever thou leadest we would go, for thy ways are perfect wisdom and love. Even when we walk through the dark valley, thy light can shine into our hearts and guide us safely through the night of sorrow. Be thou our Friend and we need ask no more in Heaven or earth, for thou art the Comfort of all who trust in thee, the Help and Defence of all who hope in thee. O Lord, we would be thine, let us never fall away from thee. We would accept all things from thy hand without murmuring, for whatever thou dost is right. Blend our wills with thine, and then we need fear no evil, nor death itself, for all things must work together for our good. Lord, keep us in thy love and truth, comfort us with thy light, and guide us by thy Holy Spirit; through Jesus Christ our Lord. Amen.

S Weiss, 1738-1805